# 25 POWER TIPS
## For The PMP® Exam
PMP EXAM PLANNING, MOTIVATION AND SUCCESS STRATEGIES

**PHILL C. AKINWALE, PMP, PMI-RMP, OPM3**

25 Power Tips for the PMP Exam
published by Praizion Media
P.O Box 22241, Mesa, AZ 85277
www.praizion.com

Author:
Phillip Akinwale, PMP, OPM3, CAPM, PMI-RMP, PMI-SP
Copyright © 2014 Praizion Media.
All rights reserved.

ISBN 978-1-934579-58-9

No part of this publication may be reproduced, transmitted in any form or by any means including but not limited to electronic, recording, manual, mechanical, recording, photograph, photocopy, or stored in any retrieval system, without the prior written permission of the publisher.

The author and publisher make no warranties or representation that use of this publication will result in passing the PMP® exam or about the completeness and accuracy of the contents. The author and publisher accept no liability, losses or damages of any kind caused or alleged to be caused directly or indirectly by this publication.

PMI®, the PMI® logo, PMBOK® and PMP® are registered marks of the Project Management Institute, Inc. Project Management Institute, *A Guide to the Project Management Body of Knowledge (PMBOK® Guide)* Fifth Edition, Project Management Institute, Inc., 2008. Copyright and all rights reserved. Material from this publication has been reproduced with the permission of PMI®.

**Printed in the United States of America**

# Table of Contents

TIP 1 – DISCARD PRECONCEIVED IDEAS .......................... 5

TIP2 – KNOW THE SYLLABUS ............................................. 17

TIP3 – KNOW THE 5-10-47 .................................................... 19

TIP4 – UNDERSTAND PAGE 61 ............................................ 20

TIP 5 – UNDERSTAND IN YOUR WORDS ......................... 21

TIP 6 – DO NOT CRAM TOOLS AND TECHNIQUES .... 22

TIP 7 – DO NOT CRAM INPUTS .......................................... 24

TIP 8 – VISIT YOUR VENUE ................................................. 25

TIP 9 – PREVIEW THE NAVIGATION ............................... 26

TIP 10 – WRITE DOWN KEY FORMULAS ........................ 27

TIP 11 – UNDERSTAND THE EXAM ................................... 29

TIP 12 – BEWARE OF "25" PRETEST Q'S ........................... 31

TIP 13 – THINK PERFORMANCE ........................................ 33

TIP 14 – PLAN TO SPEND TIME WISELY ......................... 35

TIP 15 – MAKE A CRAM SHEET .......................................... 37

TIP 16 – MAXIMIZE STUDY WITH AUDIO ...................... 39

TIP 17 – UNDERSTAND INTEGRATION ........................... 41

TIP 18 – UNDERSTAND EV FORMULAS ........................... 44

TIP 19 – STUDY CONTRACT TYPES ................................... 46

TIP 20 – READ THE CODE OF ETHICS ............................... 48

TIP 21 – PRACTICE CONSISTENTLY ................................. 50

TIP 22 – GET A GOOD NIGHT'S SLEEP ............................ 52

TIP 23 – DO NOT SECOND GUESS ................................... 55

TIP 24- STUDY WIDE ................................................................ 57

TIP 25 – CHART YOUR COURSE ........................................... 59

## TIP 1 – DISCARD PRECONCEIVED IDEAS

Throw away pre-conceived ideas about Project Management. The world of the PMI is an ideal and unique world. It is a totally different view to Project Management than what several companies practice. To succeed on this exam, you must understand Project Management from a *PMBOK® Guide* perspective.

PMBOK stands for Project Management Body of Knowledge. The Project Management Body of Knowledge Guide is the book on which the PMP exam is based. In order to succeed on this exam, you must understand the details in the thirteen (13) core chapters of the PMBOK Guide.

It is likely that you will be taking an exam based on ten (10) Knowledge Areas and five (5) Process Groups. It is very important for you to understand what these five (5) Process Groups are early in the course of your PMP exam study and also understand what the ten (10) Knowledge Areas are.

The five (5) Process Groups are:
1. Initiating
2. Planning

3. Executing
4. Monitoring and Controlling
5. Closing

The philosophy is simple; to start a project, it must be initiated. Initiating the project means, formally identifying the project, the Project Manager, the project sponsor, and any other key stakeholders who have a say in the initiating of the project. Initiating is also the authorization of the project and the Project Manager to apply resources to the project.

A project must be planned up-front for best results. The output of this is a detailed project management plan across all areas conceivable.

A project must be executed by executing the Project Management Plan developed.

Project activities must be monitored for compliance to the Project Management Plan and controlled to bring activities in-line with the Project Management Plan.

When all the deliverables have been produced and the deliverables have been officially accepted by the customer, a project must be closed and the deliverables transitioned to the customer.

The ten (10) Knowledge Areas are:
1. Project Integration Management
2. Project Scope Management
3. Project Time Management
4. Project Cost Management
5. Project Quality Management
6. Project Human Resource Management,
7. Project Communications Management,
8. Project Risk Management,
9. Project Procurement Management, and
10. Project Stakeholder Management.

*Project Integration Management*

This Knowledge Area involves understanding how the different pieces and components of Project Management come together. Think about the integration of a bicycle for example; you have the frame, the wheels, and other parts of the bicycle. Integrating those different parts form the bicycle.

In Project Integration Management, combining, uniting and coordinating different aspects of Project Management, form a well-rounded and cohesive Project Management structure.

For example, understanding how Project Scope affects Project Cost, and understanding how Project Quality could impact Project Cost, and understanding how Project Procurement Management could impact Project Cost is one small example of how different Knowledge Areas in Project Management, comes together to form a bigger well rounded picture.

The ability of Project Managers to effectively coordinate, combine and unify these prices of Project Management, makes Project Management great, or, at its best; phenomenal.

The superb Project Manager is one who understands how to coordinate, combine and unify each of the ten (10) areas of Project Management to form one big picture view, to give both stakeholders and the Project Manager, the big picture of Project Management.

Take a look at the five (5) Process Groups of Project Management; processes that fall into those five (5) groups of processes needs to be combined, unified and coordinated, and that is exactly what Project Integration Management does. It enables the Project Manager understand how to combine the different aspects of Project Management, the different processes of Project Management, the different Knowledge Areas of Project Management.

*Project Scope Management*

Scope Management deals with how to scope out a project, how to collect requirements, how to define the project scope in a detailed narrative called the Project Scope Statement. How to give a visual depiction of what the project contains; we call this the Work Breakdown Structure. The Work Break Down structure is a key part of Project Scope Management which you will be learning more about in your various Project Management course.

*Project Time Management*

Time Management involves understanding how to develop a schedule and how to control the schedule to ensure that the projects' deliverables are completed in a timely fashion.

*Project Cost Management*

Cost Management involves understanding how to estimate cost, determine the project budget by aggregating those estimates and ultimately how to control project cost.

*Project Quality Management*

Involves ensuring that the customer receives a deliverable; be it a product, a service or a result, that meets requirements and conforms to what was defined in the Requirements Traceability Matrix or Requirements Documentation.

In Quality Management, the Project Manager and the team are involved in identifying quality standards that needs to be adhered to on the project. The process of planning what needs to be adhered to, the process of constantly checking the project work through scheduled audits and the process of checking a final completed deliverable through inspection for any defects is what Project Quality Management is all about; identifying standards, checking the work processes and checking the final deliverable.

*Project Human Resource Management*

Project Human Resource Management involves planning how to acquire the project team, planning how to develop the project team and also planning how to manage the project team, taking into consideration organizational theories and other approaches to managing the project team.

Project Human Resource Management is also about actually acquiring the team, actually developing the team through team building activities, through training, through coaching and also managing the team; giving them feedback and enabling them to understand what needs to be done to achieve project success.

*Project Communications Management*

Project Communications Management involves intentionally planning how and what to communicate to stakeholders and then actually executing the plan to communicate with stakeholders at the right time when they need the information, and ensuring that all the information stakeholders need, is communicated to them; be it through manual methods, electronic methods or face-to-face.

In Project Communications Management, a Communication Management Plan is developed, then communication is generated and disseminated to stakeholders. And finally communications is controlled and if stakeholders do not receive what they need when they need it, adjustments must be made to the Communications

Management Plan to ensure that stakeholders what they need at the right time going forward.

### *Project Risk Management*

Project Risk Management is all about understanding uncertainty that could impact the project. We find uncertainties around us every day; be they possibility of weather delays, possibility of fires, and possibility of accidents. However, in Project Risk Management, we are only concerned with uncertainty that could impact the project, and that uncertainty is what the Project Manager and the team should ensure they plan for.

There is also uncertainty that is unknown. Those unknown variables are beyond what the Project Manager and the team can control. However, they can intelligently plan for uncertainties that are unknown. These are done through Management Reserves. As you study Chapter 11, be sure that you understand *Management Reserves* and *Contingency Reserves*. Also, be sure you understand the difference between *Business Risks* and *Pure Risks*. There are several terms to be discussed in Project Risk Management.

Project Risk Management involves planning how risk will be managed on the project, identifying risks, qualitatively analyzing risk, quantitatively analyzing risks, planning risk responses and monitoring and controlling risks.

*Project Procurement Management*

Project Procurement Management, in a broad sense, involves planning procurements, conducting procurements, controlling procurements and closing out the procurements.

Planning procurements; people might refer to this as managing contracts. It involves carefully considering which contract type to embark on in a unique project. After a decision has been made on which contract type to proceed with, the team is involved in sending out Request for Proposals or Request for Bids; RFPs or RFBs or IFNs, you will learn a lot of these terms. These are referred to as procurement documents, and these are used to disseminate information about the project. It is used to pass this information on to prospective sellers.

Also, in Procurement Management, the team is involved in screening the vendors or the sellers to eventually select one seller or a group of sellers, depending on the project. Through Source Selection Criteria, the team chooses whichever sellers they wish to engage on the project. After engaging the sellers on the project, after contract signed, the project team is involved in monitoring the work of these sellers and managing their efforts. This is referred to as controlling procurements. The team controls the procurement and ensures that the seller is meeting the objectives and ultimately the contracts are closed. Bear in mind that contracts with sellers are closed before the ultimate closer of the project. The ultimate closing of the project, will involve integrating between various project phases, different aspects of the project, to finally deliver the transition of the deliverable to the client or to the company involved.

The final process in Project Management is closing out the project as a whole, and this actually part of Project Integration Management; known as *Close Procurement.*

Let's discuss the final Knowledge Area in the PMBOK Guide. The final Knowledge Area is known as Project Stakeholder Management.

*Project Stakeholder Management*

As the term Stakeholder Management implies, this is where the project team is involved in managing stakeholder expectations and managing stakeholder engagement from beginning to the end. Various parts involved are:

a. Identifying Stakeholders – this is done in a formal fashion; identifying the stakeholders and documenting them in a stakeholder register.

b. Plan Stakeholder Management – the project team is involved in planning how stakeholders will be engaged on the project, how their focus and attention will be kept on the project.

c. Manage Stakeholder Engagement –in this process, the Project Manager and the team are involved in ensuring that stakeholders are engaged through carrying out those activities which were previously identified in planning.

d. Control Stakeholder Engagement – Control Stakeholder Engagement is deliberately and intentionally monitoring stakeholder engagement to ensure that stakeholders are indeed engaged; and if stakeholders are not engaged as originally planned, then adjustments must be made to the stakeholder management plan to engage these stakeholders at a deeper level on the project.

So, that concludes Tip 1: Discard Preconceived Ideas about Project Management as you can see, there are lots of aspects of Project Management that you may not carry out in the real world. The world of the PMI is an ideal and unique world; it is totally different than how Project Management is practiced in many firms because, in many firms, Project Management is practiced in an ad hoc fashion without structure and order. But, in the world of the PMI, you must understand structured project management and you must also understand the PMBOK Guide perspective.

## TIP2 – KNOW THE SYLLABUS

Understand the PMBOK Guide and the PMP exam syllabus at a high-level. This will enable you to understand the details.

We just went through Tip 1 in which we dove into the ten (10) Knowledge Areas and the five (5) Process Groups. This gave you a high-level overview of the PMBOK Guide. Doing this will enable you to better understand the material as you go along. A broad picture view of the PMBOK Guide, enables you understand how the material is woven together into a well rounded view of Project Management.

Chapters 1, 2 and 3, in the PMBOK Guide, gives you a high-level overview of Project Management core terminology. Chapters 4 -13, addresses the ten (10) Knowledge Areas and begins to dive into finer details regarding Processes, Inputs, Tools and Techniques and Outputs, and fine details of Project Management. Most of the exam is based on Chapters 4-13.

In order to get the most out of your study, it is extremely important to understand the big picture of how everything fits together.

- Understand all the Process Groups at a high-level,
- Understand all the Knowledge Areas at a high-level, and
- Understand all the Processes at a high-level

What I have realized is that when students understand the big picture how things fit together and how are defined at a macro level, going down to a micro level becomes easier. They absolutely understand what each Knowledge Area, Process Groups or Process is meant to achieve. With that understanding, how it is achieved, becomes easier to understand. The Inputs make more sense. The Tools and Techniques make more sense and the Outputs make more sense. Inputs, Tools and Techniques and Outputs, form the granular pieces of the PMBOK Guide, but before you understand the granular bits; understand the macro bits.

## TIP3 – KNOW THE 5-10-47

Understand how Project Management is broken down into five (5) Process Groups and ten (10) Knowledge Areas. Also understand how this is broken down further into forty-seven (47) unique processes.

To get a good picture of this, I suggest looking at page 61 in the *PMBOK® Guide* Fifth Edition. This shows you all the processes under each Process Group, and all the processes under each Knowledge Area. I would strongly suggest understanding the table on page 61 and being able to draw out that table; not from memory purely, but really with an understanding of how the different processes relate to each other, how the processes in each Knowledge Area relate amongst themselves and how the processes in each Process Groups are relevant to each other and how they inter-relate amongst themselves.

# TIP 4 – UNDERSTAND PAGE 61

Understand page 61 in the PMBOK® Guide Fifth edition. This page is key in understanding how each process maps back to a Knowledge Area and a Process Group.

Several test takers start off their exam by doing a "brain-dump" of this table to build confidence and rationalize process relationships on any questions that require it. Others choose to go straight to the questions but nonetheless this exercise of drawing out the table on page 61 will get you in to the proverbial "PMP zone".

## TIP 5 – UNDERSTAND IN YOUR WORDS

Ensure that you know all the processes in the PMBOK® Guide and that you can explain them accurately in your own words. For the exam, you should be able to apply all processes to a real project and identify proper and improper process steps.

## TIP 6 – DO NOT CRAM TOOLS AND TECHNIQUES

Tools and Techniques need not be crammed. Instead, you should UNDERSTAND what exactly they are and what they are used for in the processes where they appear.

Understand the application of these Tools; understand the application of these Techniques and their relevance to the process at hand.

To get a good idea of what a Tool or Technique is; it is extremely important that you visualize that Tool or Technique. You might use a white board and chart out what exactly that Tool or Technique does for you; regardless of the Knowledge Area.

For example, in Quality Management knowledge area, there are seven basic Quality tools and seven Quality Management tools. These need to be understood and visualized; for that reason, I would advise that you visit a website such as ASQ's website (www.asq.org) and find these Tools and Techniques of Quality. Do the same for all the other Tools and Techniques in Project Management documented in the PMBOK Guide.

When you actually visualize these Tools, or you have resources such as asq's website that go into more detail regarding the practical application of these Tools to a process or to a business, it becomes very clear what exactly they are; what they are used for. And from knowing them in that level of detail, you are able to rule out options given to you on questions that are wrong or that have nothing to do with the process at hand. For that reason, I advise, understanding Tools as opposed to cramming Tools and Techniques!

## TIP 7 – DO NOT CRAM INPUTS

Inputs and outputs need not be crammed. You should UNDERSTAND what they are and where they originate from. Also, understand why certain Outputs become Inputs to a process; understand where certain Inputs to a process come from.

Certain Inputs, for example – the business case, come from outside the project. You must understand where such Inputs come from because not every single Input comes from a process within the forty-seven (47) processes.

So understand where things outside the project come from and that will greatly help you understand it. I would also suggest that you look for examples of documents like the business case or understand what is in an MOU; a Memorandum of Understanding or a LOI; a Letter of Intent. Understand these types of documents that are either explicit Inputs such as the business case or implicit Inputs such as LOIs and MOUs and contracts, which are part of agreements, which is an Input to Develop Project Charter for example.

## TIP 8 – VISIT YOUR VENUE

Visit your exam venue before the day of the exam. You certainly do not want to get to the exam center late or not be able to find it on your exam day. This has actually happened to students in the past. Can you imagine getting to your exam venue late? That would create a lot of stress and it could contribute to unsatisfactory performance.

Also, you should call the day before your exam and be sure that all systems are up and running. Exam center shutdowns are not uncommon. This actually happened to students of mine in the USA and the UK. One student drove 80 miles only to be told the exam center was closed due to weather incidents in the Virginia area. The other student in the UK, also drove over 100 miles to the exam center, travelled for over 3 hours, only to be told the exam testing system had a glitch. Consequently, he had to drive back over 100 miles and return 2 weeks later.

Such incidences are not always preventable, but in some cases, calling the day before the exam, could be a big help.

## TIP 9 – PREVIEW THE NAVIGATION

There is a short demo before the exam that teaches you how to use the exam interface and navigate through the questions presented to you. This shows you how to skip questions, mark questions and navigate as you need to. I advise you to watch our video about this on YouTube. You can find this video at www.tiny.cc/pmpscreen. It will save you lots of time in trying to wrap your head around how the navigation system works; even though it is fairly straight forward. This saves timed time can be put to good use on the exam.

## TIP 10 – WRITE DOWN KEY FORMULAS

I suggest that once you have watched the demo on how to navigate through the exam's interface, spend any unused time you have, writing down the key formulas, key tables and key points that you feel will be useful on the exam. Some students feel this is not a vital step; whereas other students say, without this step, they would not have done as great on either the PMP or the CAPM exam as they did.

The reason is, when you get into the heart of the exam, very quickly, this key information could dissipate from your head, and to prevent that, write this information down before you start the exam.

Different people have different test habits and we all feel differently under certain conditions in an exam room. Once you have written down the key formulas; be it for Earned Value, TCPI, Future Value, Planned Value, what have you; at least you know you have those formulas down and you will not forget them as the exam questions may scramble your understanding a little bit.

Some people go as far as drawing out page 61; the table that has the five (5) Process Groups, ten (10)

Knowledge Areas and forty-seven (47) Processes. To some, it might be overkill; but I've heard many a client's tell me that it helped get them into the "PMP Zone" and affirm their understanding a few minutes before hitting the start button for the exam proper.

## TIP 11 – UNDERSTAND THE EXAM

The PMP exam consists of two hundred (200) multiple choice questions. These questions are randomly generated from a huge question database. The examinee must choose one (1) correct answer from four (4) options. There is no negative marking on the exam.

Note however that not all questions carry the same weight; some questions carry a greater weight than others. However the specific weighting criterion is not known. But with this information in hand, you could understand why a question could take you upwards of three (3) minutes and other questions could take you twenty (20) seconds. So don't expect all the questions to be weighted the same way and don't expect to feel the same level of stress, when answering all the questions.

Have an even pace as you move through the exam, spending time on questions you know are important to you and you can answer; as opposed to questions that you think are important, but you cannot conveniently answer.

Typically, I do not spend more than two (2) minutes on a question. If I've spent more than two (2) minutes trying to get to the depth of the question, then it probably means it's a good time for me to mark that question, take a best guess, just in case I do not have time at the exam, and move on.

If I do have time at the end of the exam, to spend on questions like that, then I spend the last minute of the exam on those questions. But you do need to understand the break out of the exam to know how to wisely use your time; how to ensure that you sufficiently answer enough correct questions. There is no point spending five (5) or ten (10) minutes on question 10, and holding up question 200 or question 198 that you can answer.

On my exam, it was a key decision I made, not to stay stumped on questions 1-20, but to move further ahead to questions downstream that enabled me to pass the test. So understand the makeup of the exam and spend time planning how to work around the exam.

## TIP 12 – BEWARE OF "25" PRETEST Q's

Out of the two hundred (200) questions on the PMP exam, there are twenty-five (25) questions that are randomly distributed, and these specific twenty-five (25) questions are known as Pretest Questions.

These Pretest Questions do not count. These are not used for scoring purposes; instead, these are used more for data-gathering purposes. Since these questions are not distinguishable from the other questions, you must answer ALL two hundred (200) questions to the best of your ability.

Regardless how much you have prepared for the PMP exam, be aware that there are questions you have no clue about. Do not let these bother you. Move along quickly because these could derail you if you waste time on them.

Reading directly from the PMP Handbook regarding these 25 Pretest Questions it says, on page 17:

*"A PMP examination is comprised of two hundred (200) multiple choice questions. Of the two hundred (200) questions, twenty five (25) are considered Pretest Questions. Pretest Questions do not affect the score and are used in examinations as*

*an effective and legitimate way to test the validity of future examination questions. All questions are randomly placed throughout the examination. The number of Pretest questions is twenty five (25), the total examination questions are two hundred (200) and the allotted examination time is four (4) hours."*

The twenty five (25) Pretest Questions are a signal to the PMI regarding the degree or nature of the average students' preparation. The key takeaway point is; there are likely to be questions that you cannot conveniently answer or that you have no clue about. Be prepared to face these.

## TIP 13 – THINK PERFORMANCE

The PMP exam passing score is unknown. This means that test takers must aim for the highest possible score, leaving no stone unturned; as opposed to just trying to "get by".

What do I mean by "the passing score is unknown"? When you are done with your PMP exam, you will receive a printed copy of your test results in addition to your overall pass or fail status. But realize that the PMI defines levels of proficiency as follow:

1. *Proficient* in a Process Group indicates that your performance is above the average level of knowledge in that Process Group.
2. *Moderately Proficient* indicates that your performance is at the average level of knowledge in that Process Group.
3. *Below Proficient* indicates that your performance is below the average level of knowledge in that Process Group.

For people who pass the exam, the performance information will help identify chapters or areas to focus on for continuing education purposes. So in other words, if you pass the PMP exam, but there are areas that you did not do sufficiently well on the exam, this could be an area that you focus on when gathering your professional development unit for your PMP exam maintenance.

So, since the PMP exam is not based on a score, and it is more based on attaining a certain overall level of proficiency, then it makes sense when taking the exam to be focused on performance; your optimum performance. Not answering just enough questions to get by, but aiming for the absolute success at the very highest grade.

The exam scoring method is based on the Angoff method. Read a little bit more about the Angoff method by visiting the link: **http://www.tinyurl.com/angoff**. Go to that link and read more about the Angoff method; it will give you a clearer picture of how the PMI come out with a health passing range.

Scores per domain or Process Group are no longer provided. Instead, the PMI provide a report of exam performance; as I said, you are graded based on the three (3) categories; you are either, Proficient, Moderately Proficient or Below Proficient in a particular Process Group. So think of optimum performance.

## TIP 14 – PLAN TO SPEND TIME WISELY

The PMP exam is four (4) hours in duration, so spend all your time wisely. There is no point using less than 4 hours on the exam, only to fail the exam; so use all the available time as needed. All the time is meant to be used, so take your time.

Take the exam by taking mental breaks when needed; take the exam by going to the rest-room as needed. Have a snack or drink from the water fountain.

A student of mine actually went as far as taking three (3) breaks on his four (4) hour exam. Well needless to say, he got certified; he is now a PMP, and shared that information with one of our classes.

I found his strategy to be rather interesting and decided to give it a try on my Risk Management Professional exam. I took three (3) calculated breaks at specific points.

On the first break, I doused my head with water in a restroom when my head was overheating due to those tough risk questions. On my second break, I took a bio-break; and on my third break, I went to the water fountain to have a very refreshing drink of water. I felt fresher than ever. I was able to take my exam in a peaceful and stress free manner by taking three (3) breaks spread across those hours.

I would highly suggest to anyone who has more than enough time on their hands, perhaps due to the fact that they are very quick reading questions and answering questions, to take breaks as needed. Don't rush the exam; but spread it out, take your time, take mental breaks, and you'll find yourself performing at a much higher efficiency as you build it into your test.

## TIP 15 – MAKE A CRAM SHEET

Use cram-sheets and cheat-sheets while studying for the exam to rapidly gain and consolidate key knowledge. Spend time creating your own cheat-sheets with areas that may be uncommon to you highlighted. Write out definitions to ITTOs in your own words, after carrying out further study or research on any unfamiliar terms.

There is so much information in the PMBOK Guide that it would make sense to condense those tough definitions that you have had trouble with. Remember it's the 20% that you are unfamiliar with or do not study that could hurt you on 80% of the exam. It's just like the 80:20 rule all over again; 20% of your weak areas are responsible for 80% of your failures. So, we need to be aware of that and prevent this from happening.

I would suggest creating a cheat-sheet or cram-sheet by digging into the unknown detail; those details that you are not comfortable with. Gain a well-rounded understanding of them and document them in your own words for future recall.

A good cram-sheet should not have every single definition but those that you clearly are having trouble with. Also the cheat-sheet should not be a mini-PMBOK, but it should have select portions of it that are peculiar to your own specific needs.

Don't waste time summarizing the known! Go for the unknown. Go for the dark, cloudy and unknown content when creating your summary. Use buzz words and catch phrases and easy to recall sentences. Let me give you an example; the Delphi Technique. The key words in this definition for the Delphi Technique are **Anonymous** and **Experts**. Those are the key words that help you recall the full definition of the Delphi Technique; Anonymous and Experts. That could trigger the whole paragraph coming back to mind, and that's exactly what you need to do when you are creating your cheat-sheet. Look for those buzz words that will help you recall the full definition without writing out an entire paragraph.

## TIP 16 – MAXIMIZE STUDY WITH AUDIO

Use audio study guides such as The Project Management Audio Digest to study for the exam. You can listen to these CDs while driving, while doing chores or working out. Audio CDs and MP3s enable you to maximize time by multi-tasking.

The key to getting the most from audio is active listening, deliberate listening and repeated listening.

To listen actively, as you listen, try to join the pieces of Project Management information you already know together with what you are listening to.

To deliberately listen, every few minutes, call your attention back to the content and ask yourself – what was just said or ask yourself, what did I hear that is most relevant to applying this knowledge to the real world?

To repeatedly listen, listen to a CD again, and again, and again, until you can almost hear what's coming next as you listen to it.

Audio study, for those who gravitate towards it, could greatly save you time during your study. If you have a thirty (30) minute commute to work and a thirty (30) minute commute back, you could spend that valuable time listening to audio, to top up your knowledge and get you in the right zone for studying that you will do either later on in the day or later on at night when you are done with work.

The payoff of intentional use of audio is really enormous. I have had students tell me, they listened to my audio CDs several times a day, and it gets to the point that they know the information so well, that they don't need to read it endlessly in a book.

## TIP 17 – UNDERSTAND INTEGRATION

Understand the Project Integration Management knowledge area. Why should I do that exclusively? Because it is a very unique area.

This Knowledge Area addresses the integration of all Project Management processes. It talks about how they are unified, combined and united.

For example, Perform Integrated Change Control process involves interactivity between all of the processes in the Monitoring and Controlling process group.

Think about it, as you are carrying out Integrated Change Control, you need to integrate all of the different Change Requests from all of the different processes, especially those from the Monitoring and Controlling process group; and you need to come out with either Approval or Rejection, and you need to update the Change Log. So there is a lot of integration going on. But if you don't read in between the lines of integration, it will seem to be like any other Knowledge Area.

Project Integration Management is a very unique Knowledge Area, in that, it combines all of the processes across the ten (10) Knowledge Areas and five (5) Process Groups. So you do need to spend a little bit more time in Integration to understand the granularity.

Let's take another look at why we should study Integration on a deeper level. If you take a look at two (2) processes within Integration; which are Develop Project Charter and Close Project and Phase.

If you observe the percentage from those two (2) Process Groups that those processes fall in, you'll realize that Develop Project Charter could very well be, roughly, 6 ½% of your exam and Close Project or Phase could very well account for 4% of your exam; because there are two (2) processes in Initiating, where develop Project Charter is, and Initiating is 13% of the exam. In the same vein, in the Closing process group, where Close Project or Phase is, you have 8% at stake. So if you divide both of those numbers by 2, you have 6 ½ and 4. That's 10.5% of the exam, if you are to look at it that way; from just 2 processes in Integration.

Now what happens when you dig into all of the other processes across Integration? You very quickly realize that it all adds up. Even more important is the possibility of a loaded question; I call them loaded because you could be tested from the perspective of Time, Cost and Scope all in one question. And this is where Integration comes in. You need to understand how all of the processes in a question, integrate; how they influence each other.

For that reason, Project Integration Management is a foundation on which several other processes are built from. So spend time and know it well.

## TIP 18 – UNDERSTAND EV FORMULAS

Know all earned value formulas and the rationale for computing the following: Earned Value (EV), Actual Cost (AC), Planned Vale (PV), Cost Variance (CV), Schedule Variance (SV), Schedule Performance Index (SPI), Cost Performance Index (CPI), Budget at Completion (BAC), Estimate at Completion (EAC) (based on all 4 different scenarios documented in the PMBOK Guide), Variance at Completion (VAC) and TCPI. Be sure to understand what the different values that you derive from these earned value formulas actually mean.

For example, on a 15 month project with equally broken out work portions per month, what is the BAC if for month 6, SPI is 5 and CPI is 0.5. Actual cost spent for month 6 is: $500,000.

Write that out on paper and see what you come out with. What is the BAC?

To solve this problem, you must be familiar with the formulas for CPI and SPI. Working backwards using these formulas, you can find out what exactly the Planned Value is, and once you know what the Planned Value is for a particular month, you multiply that by the 15 months work period, and from there, you derive your BAC.

On the exam, you will not always be given the Earned Value value, you may need to calculate that yourself as in this problem.

The answer to the problem is $750,000.00 for BAC; because BAC is Cumulative Planned Value. So try to see these problems on Earned Value as one piece of several puzzles. On the exam, questions may not always be as direct as what is the SPI or CPI based on very finite criteria. You may be given lots of Red Herrings that could make you deviate down Alleys that are blind Alleys, leading you to wrong choices form among those choices which the PMI have deliberately listed, knowing that people will fall into the incorrect formula application trap.

So, know these formulas as good as you can; not cramming them. Cramming doesn't mean knowing; knowing means being able to apply it in a wide variety of scenarios.

## TIP 19 – STUDY CONTRACT TYPES

Know all contract types as well as their pros and cons. There are three (3) broad categories of contracts:

1. Fixed Price Contracts
2. Cost Reimbursable Contracts
3. Time and Materials Contracts

Depending on the nature of work being done, any of these three (3) contract types could be the most favourable. Also depending on whom you are in the question, Buyer or Seller, any of those three (3) contract types could be most preferred. Under Fixed Priced Contracts, we have:

- Fixed Price Incentive Fee,
- Firm Fixed Price; and
- Fixed Price with Economic Price Adjustment.

Consider a question that asks you which contract would you select if you were a Vendor that had a multi-year contract, spanning across several decades with an organization. Would you choose a Fixed Price Incentive Fee contract, a Fixed Price with Economic Price Adjustment contract or a Firm Fixed Price contract? You do need to know what each of these contracts have to offer to make a right decision.

Under Cost Reimbursable Contracts, we have:
- Cost Plus Incentive Fee
- Cost Plus Award Fee
- Cost Plus Fixed Fee.

Go into the details and understand the differences between each of these Cost Reimbursable Contracts. The Cost plus Award Fee is probably the most subjective of them all. But understand why and the definitions for the others.

The final contract is Time and Materials contract, which is a hybrid of Fixed Price and Cost Reimbursable. Get prepared to find many questions regarding procurements and contracts on the exam.

The Plan Procurement Management process has several inputs, but the contract types lie in a recurring theme which we've seen so many times. The contract types are discussed in Organizational Process Assets, which is an Input to Plan Procurement Management.

For this reason, pay close attention to the Organizational Process Assets talked about in this section of the PMBOK Guide.

## TIP 20 – READ THE CODE OF ETHICS

Know the responsibilities of the Project Manager and read both the PMI Code of Ethics and Professional Conduct and also the PMP Exam Content Outline.

I suggest that Project Managers don't just read the PMBOK and the study Guide but also understand the Code of Ethics; because these Code of Ethics code be baked into the questions on the exam, and if you haven't studied the Code Ethics, you might be a bit surprised at the nature of questions you could be asked.

A lot of these questions border on what the right thing is for the Project Manager to do from a very PMI-centered perspective. Some of the questions and answers may come as a surprise to someone who has not really understood and digested the PMI Code of Ethics and Professional Conduct. So read this document and get prepared to face questions that may be difficult in the way they are posed and in the options that they present.

In addition to reading this free PMI issued document, I would also recommend that you study and read the PMP Exam Content Outline. Read it again, and again to understand what the contents of the exam are, the way the questions have been set up and the way the exam have been structured as a whole. The payoff of doing this could be rather significant on your test. So, study the blueprint in the PMP exam content outline.

To find either of these documents, Google the term: PMP Exam Handbook, for the Handbook; and PMP Exam Content Outline, for the Content Outline.

## TIP 21 – PRACTICE CONSISTENTLY

Practice, practice, practice and find gaps in your Project Management reasoning and knowledge. Practice with simulation exams and tests to find these gaps before they find you on the exam. The more questions you answer the better or let me say, the more good questions you answer, the better. The thought provoking question you answer, the better. Because, they are different types of exams.

Nowadays, there are so many free exams out there that it is hard to separate what is good from what is not. It is hard to separate what should not even be out there from what should. I would suggest going with a registered education provider that has been tested and tried in more ways than one. I would also suggest going with courses that have been tested and tried by other PMs and have a good success rate on the PMP exam. I would also suggest taking quizzes and tests that several people have validated and verified.

Using faulty questions to practice could prove to be very detrimental on the exam, in that it could give you preconceived ideas of how easy the exam appears to be, when the exam is actually a lot more difficult than the questions you are answering.

I have come across students who are absolutely shocked at the difficulty level of the test only because they used a certain system that promised a certain degree of ease on the exam.

Practice consistently, but practice with reliable, tested and tried materials.

## TIP 22 – GET A GOOD NIGHT'S SLEEP

Sleep early the day before the exam especially if your exam is in the morning. If you are not fully prepared for the PMP exam at 6.00PM the day before the exam, the reality is, there is very little that last minute cramming can do.

The exam tests your understanding of PMBOK Guide principles more than anything else. So, if you have not embraced the philosophy and you do not understand how to apply the knowledge and the principles in the PMBOK Guide sufficiently, at 6 PM the day before your exam, there is very little that an extra day can do.

For this reason, front load your schedule. Study ahead of time so that the night before the exam, you can get a very good night sleep and have a relaxed mind. In fact, I tell my students the day before the exam, come 6 PM, you should find yourself shutting it down, and later on that night, you want to do something fun like watch a movie, watch a comedy; one of my students watched a Jackie Chan movie the night before his exam. Another of my student watched Monsters University the night before her exam. They both pass with great grades. In fact, one of my students, Sarah got

4 proficients out of 5 watching Monsters University the day before her exam.

You see, it's not in stressing yourself out in the dying hours, it's all about front loading your schedule and studying intelligently, making sure you have crossed all of those "T's" and dotted those "I's" before 6PM the night before your exam. This is so important.

I have also seen students fail as a result of over studying; studying till the wee hours of the morning, only to find that they have got a brain freeze and they cannot function effectively in the exam. They find out that they have studied so much that they cannot read the questions without the noise getting in the way.

Sleeping early before your exam is critical for your success. Have a reliable study plan, and the night before the exam, you'll be laughing all the way to sleep and waking up to ace the test.

Now the question might come up, well, "I have got my exam at 5PM the next day. What time should I shut it down?" I still maintain that you should shut it down early. If you have your exam 5PM /6PM the next day, I don't expect to see you studying 8PM or 9PM the night before; by 7PM, I would definitely have shut it down.

I have taken five PMI certification exams and when you count my OPM3 in which I took several exams, I can tell you that you are either ready or you are not. And studying incessantly all the way up to the exam is only a failure waiting to happen. Be wise, get a good night sleep.

## TIP 23 – DO NOT SECOND GUESS

DO NOT second guess yourself on the PMP exam; it is one of the biggest killers of success.

Have you ever taken a test and have a gut feeling that a particular answer was the right one but for one reason or the other, which I will call second guessing, you end up choosing something else, only to find out at the end of the test that you were right the first time.

This is what happens when you second guess. It is a proven fact. So avoid changing your initial answer to any other answer on the exam except you are 100% sure that you were wrong the first time; because there are instances on my test where I was absolutely wrong the first time, but I remembered a key definition or a key fact that made me change my initial answer on a question to something new.

There are times that happens and you know that you are right the second time; 100%. If that is not the case, don't change your first answer. Don't change your first answer unless you are 100% sure that you have remembered key points in determining the correct answer.

People who second guess themselves all the way through the exam; have a higher likelihood of failure. So learn to be confident in what you answer. At the end of the day, it boils down to habit. Study great, take a lot of great test, but practice the art of not second guessing. It's an art and it needs practice. The more practice you get of it, the more confident you will become of your gut instinct. And the more confident you become regarding your gut instinct, the less likely you are to change your correct answer and fail the test.

## TIP 24- STUDY WIDE

Taking an exam like the PMP exam could be a challenge if you have not studied enough. And by not studying enough, I am not talking about the duration or the time put into studying; I am talking about content.

For the PMP exam, you do need to study wide within the relevant areas that are talked about in the PMP Exam Content Outline. This is a freely available document which you can download.

Google the term PMP Exam Content Outline and then read the outline, read it page by page and any areas that are uncommon to you need to be read both in the *PMBOK®* Guide and in any additional documentation from a reliable source; be it a book on the PMIs Books 24x7 or any other source that clearly defines what the PMI have listed as an exam component.

For exam, if you take a look at the Performance Domain 2, for the Planning process group in this document on page 6, look at task 8; it states: *develop a quality management plan based on the project scope and requirements in order to prevent the occurrence of defects and reduce the cost of quality*. Reading through task 8 on page 6, if I was studying for the exam, I would read wide to understand what each of those things mentioned is. *The Quality Management Plan. What is Project Scope? What are Requirements? Occurrence of Defects and Cost of Quality* that has so many things mentioned in it and so do all the other tasks in this document.

To read wide, understand every single term, leave no stone unturned in understanding all the terms mentioned in the PMP Exam Content Outline. Read them in the Glossary, in the Lexicon of Terms, read wide and ensure you have a good understanding of all the content from various angles.

## TIP 25 – CHART YOUR COURSE

Chart your course to PMP Exam Success! This is by far the most important of all tips because all the other tips can be used to do this.

Charting your course involves having a plan for each aspect of the PMP Exam. Let's break down the PMP exam into four (4) different pieces:

1. Power tips for the PMP Exam application strategy
2. PMP Exam 35 Contact Hour Course
3. Studying for the PMP Exam
4. PMP Exam

I also have a 5th section which applies to after the exam, what to do after getting PMP certified (key tips and ideas)

### 1. PMP Exam application strategy

This is one of the most difficult aspects of the PMP Exam, putting your exam application together and documenting your experience. Lots of PMs complain about how difficult it is to get either the 4500 hours documented or the 7500 hours documented. The first thing you want to do for your PMP Exam strategy is:

1. *Read the handbook* Read the PMP Handbook in detail. Reading the Handbook will enable you to see the big picture view of what the PMI is looking for from you in the application and also on the exam. Not reading the Handbook first before anything else, could lead you on several wrong paths and ultimately failure. So the most important thing before doing anything else is to understand the exam you are getting into by reading the Handbook, studying the requirements and understanding the best way possible.

2. *Schedule your application prep* on your calendar to really get it done. I went through problems after my PMP Exam taking my next PMI exam. And the way I got it done, was deciding on a particular weekend to lock myself in a room for 8 hours and I would not come out until I got the application done. That's how I does my PMI-SP and PMI-RMP applications

completed. These applications had been hanging for months. In fact, I had gotten calls from the PMI saying "aren't you going to complete your application? It's hanging. We are going to have to archive it and you are going to have to re-open it again." You don't want that to happen. You want to schedule your application prep on your calendar and get it done in a timely fashion.

3. <u>Get in touch with people from your past, from previous employments</u>: managers, colleagues and customers. Get in touch with these people intentionally, because these could be your contacts on your PMP Exam application that help verify or validate your experience. I remember I had to contact my boss from a previous employment in the UK telling him I would use him as a Reference, as a contact on my application. That's exactly what you want to start doing early.

4. <u>Take time out to get everything done.</u> If you don't take time out to intentionally get your

application done, no one else is going to get it done for you; this is all about you. When you have everything done except your 35 contact hours, keep the application ready for the completion of your PMP Exam course. So, submit your application when you have completed your 35 contact hours. At this point, the PMI will not ask you for payment so there is nothing to be afraid of in submitting your application when you are done, when the requirements are complete, because you will not be asked to pay at that point. Some people are also concerned that their one year duration to take the Exam will start ticking the moment they submit the application. But that is not the case. The one hour period, within which you can take the exam, only starts after your application has been approved. So do not worry about that.

2. **PMP Exam 35 Contact Hour Course**

These are tips on taking your PMP Exam 35 Contact Hour Course or if you are going for less than 35 contact hours, these tips can also help you.

1. <u>Thoroughly research</u> the company, course and most importantly the Instructor. The Instructor is by far the most important piece of the puzzle when you are taking a course. If you have a great Instructor with a great track record and one who really demonstrates that track record in class, one who cares about your success; the payoff is huge.

2. <u>Use a Registered Education Provider</u> (R.E.P) where possible. The reason is because REPs have gone through vetting and validation through a PMI process. So, REPs have been found to uphold certain standards. I would advise, use an REP.

3. <u>Go for a course where you can solve a lot of problems and discuss the real-world application of the knowledge</u>. You don't need a talking head to stand in front of you regurgitating slides

behind him or her or what's in the PMBOK. You need someone who has been there, done that and who can take all of that knowledge, all of that information and bring it to life in your industry, in a language that you understand. And if you do not have that level of interaction from an Instructor, that pragmatic aspect of training, I strongly advise you to look elsewhere.

4. <u>Use your instructor as a mentor</u> if possible, otherwise; look for one. Look for an Instructor or a Mentor who teaches on a regular basis with evidence of helping people get PMP certified. Yes, I know it's all about you being determined for yourself, but many a time, I have inspired students to pick themselves up from where they left themselves and get the job done. Sometimes it takes someone on your team pushing you over the brink of success into success itself; and that is why I strongly recommend an Instructor as a Mentor or someone else as a Mentor to help you.

5. *Schedule the course at a convenient time.* Don't schedule it when you are going through bereavement, when you have a lot on your mind, when the job is totally overwhelming you and you know that you will have no breathing space when you come out. No! No! No! You don't want to take the course at such a time; you want to take a course at a convenient time where you have company backing, you have no too much on your plate and you are able to process the information you are hearing so that you can ask meaningful questions and absorb the information. You also need to prepare yourself psychologically for your PMP Exam course, especially if it is 5 day, 35 contact hour's course. It could be very intense, so take your course seriously: no phones, emails or interruptions.
6. *Ask questions. Don't be afraid of looking clueless.* Clueless is good before the test and not after.
7. *Listen and ask questions more than write.* Take notes only when you absolutely needed to or when you've got an 'ah-ha' moment or when there is

key information that you absolutely need to write down. Otherwise, if you are in right PMP Exam course, you should have lots of the information discussed, already catalogued in a study guide. So, only write when you absolutely need to. Spend more time thinking, paying attention, asking questions, being in the heart of the moment.

8. *Solve as many good tough problems as possible.* Note, not as many tough problems as possible; but as many **good** tough problems as possible. Because there are lots of tough PMP problems out there in the world of 'free PMP exams materials', but not all of them are good. Some of them are absolutely, ridiculously tough from a perspective that has nothing to do with the PMI but more to do with a particular field within the Knowledge Areas. Some questions are tailored such that only a professional in that field could answer them and those questions are not realistic. Questions that take you far off PMP course, all in a bit to pose difficulty, are not worth consideration. Be careful

the questions you take. Solve as many good tough problems as possible.

3. **PMP Exam Study**

For your PMP Exam study:

1. *Have a schedule.* Stay on it even when you miss. If you have purchased this book or MP3. Send in an email to ask for my Seven System Study Plan. My Seven System Study Plan can be used with my DVDs, CDs, Study Guide, Flashcards, Online system, mentoring and so on. So, if you are a student, make sure you ask for that timetable. You can also Google the Seven Systems Study Plan or search on YouTube and you will find this plan in my videos. Stay on the plan even when you miss, whether you are using the Seven System Study Plan or another plan, stay on the plan.

2. *Be rugged and dogged.* Be prepared to fight to get it done. Don't think there will be distractions, because there will be! There will be projects to attend to! There will be friends

and families and life to attend to. So you do need to be prepared to fight!

3. <u>As you study, don't just study in a linear fashion by Knowledge Area.</u> So many people only study down the Knowledge Areas, they forget the interactions between processes by Process Group and at random. Processes do not always interact in the order of Knowledge Areas. They do not always interact going from one process to the other within either the process group column or the Knowledge Area row. This is so important to realize. Project Management is not linear. So read at random, take various processes and read them, overlapping into Knowledge Areas and Process Groups. For example, I could read Develop Project Charter today and tomorrow, I could read Identify Stakeholders and the next day I could read Plan Stakeholder Management and the next day I could read Close Project or Phase; read out of order. That will help you be agile; it will help you weave the different pieces, the

different dependencies of Project Management together. Such that when you find questions, you don't have to ramp up to get in knowledge area mode or process group mode, it will all be Project Management to you, however the PMI pose it.

4. *Keep it balanced:* Read, solve lots of problems, study templates and tools, use templates and tools, watch videos, listen to lessons learned, speak with a mentor, teach other people, use flashcards, use audio CDs and you can even make your flashcards, you can practice brain-dumping key information to get warmed up if that helps you. There are so many ways you can keep it balanced and if you have Apps for the PMP Exam Prep, be it on an Android Phone like we've got Android Apps, if you go to Google play or Amazon and search for them, you could use those Apps. There are so many things that you could use to keep it balanced. Don't just read, read, read; or solve problems, solve problems, solve problems; do

various things, have discussions, go to study groups, have a study buddy; many things you could do.

5. As the day approaches, I would suggest <u>using more cheat-sheets and summaries</u>. Practice reading the information fast. Practice makes perfect.

6. I would also suggest that you <u>visit the exam venue before your exam.</u>

7. <u>Leave no stone unturned</u> in the things you do to get prepared for the test.

8. Do not take it for granted that <u>several things may not show up</u>. You know who people sometimes say, oh network diagrams didn't come out in my exam, probably it won't in your; don't listen to that. You never know what's coming down the pike on the PMP Exam.

9. I would also suggest that you <u>join a study group or form one</u> or have a study buddy and motivate each other towards PMP exam success!

10. *Practice answering exam questions in both quiet and in noise.* Practice answering exam questions by taking a break in between with the clock still running. Practice going for breaks, practice having a snack in the middle of your test. These distractions and quite, which for some people is a distraction will help you cope with the oscillating exam conditions; one minute it's noisy, next minute it's quite. One minute's it's quite, next minute it's noisy. Sometime you might find yourself needing to go for a bio-break whether you planned for it or not, you find yourself having to go. So practice getting into the mode of interruption. It will help you greatly on your test.

4. **PMP Exam**
    1. *Deliberate, intentional planning,* which is why we are listening to this in the first place. But to be more specific, plan breaks on your exam. If you are someone who needs to take a break, plan your breaks in. And if you feel like you don't

need a break or that you do better not taking breaks, be prepared to face the consequence of not taking breaks. Because not taking breaks means that you are going full throttle from beginning to end. It could be pretty intense! My first PMI exam was my PMP exam and I did not take a break. Not taking a break doesn't mean being efficient; so, if you do not take a break, understand that there could be a tradeoff there in efficiency. I have taken PMI exams taking no breaks and taking three (3) breaks. And I found, when I took 3 breaks on my Risk Managemnet Exam, I had a huge payoff in that I came back and I was totally refreshed the first time, went for the second break, totally refreshed again, came back for the third break and I was so refreshed that I had over an hour left on my exam. It became so easy to answer the questions by taking the edge off the intensity. So be wise when you are planning your breaks. If you plan to take a break, as I said in the last set of tips, practice that before the test.

2. *Know your average velocity* on reliable & difficult tests. By velocity I mean how many questions you answer within a particular hour or the exam as a whole. What's your rate of question answering? Have an idea of that. And as you go through the exam, try to be aware of how much time you are spending per question. One of the worst things that could happen to anyone on the exam is to space out answering difficult questions which you feel you can answer, only to get to 3:59:59 seconds and realize you didn't even have the chance to answer all the questions. You have 15 or 20 left! That is not an ideal on the PMP exam. The ideal situation is that you know your velocity and you see it coming. One hour left and you can see that if you don't do something drastic there is no way you can finish the exam; but you want to be able to see it before it happens. You don't want to get to 3:59:59 and you

see...too late, you see the countdown timing you out of the exam as it happened on one of my exams by the way. You don't want that to happen you. So, know your velocity, plan ahead.

3. *Beware of noise.* On the exam, there will be the typewriting exam going on in some test centers, there will be people coughing; one of my students named a lady in the test center; Mrs. Cough because she coughed and coughed until he could take it no more and he put his head phones on to block out the noise.

4. *Focus on winning.* There will be times when you feel weak on the exam, especially if you had not have enough sleep and you might find yourself questioning your ability to pass; at that point, focus on winning. Tell yourself you can do it. Hit those questions hard with all of your attention because YOU CAN DO IT!

5. *Answer as many questions as you can correctly. - Find your gimmes!*

6. Some people really have bad test anxiety. <u>Find ways of taking care of this feeling</u>. Just remember, the people who wrote the questions are Project Managers just like you. The people who wrote the questions spent considerable time, probably in teams, talking about one question and that's why if you've put a lot of time and energy into your prep, when you get into the exam, just remember all the great work you've done and don't be afraid of those questions because you can do it! If I could do it; you can do it! If 500,000 people in the world have done it, then you can truly succeed.

7. <u>Be dogged, be rugged and don't be scared</u>.

Talking about PMs who've been dogged and rugged, maybe this is your 2$^{nd}$ attempt, or 3$^{rd}$ or 4$^{th}$ or 5$^{th}$, it doesn't matter. I have made PMS who passed on their 1$^{st}$ attempt, those who passed on their 4$^{th}$.

One thing is the same though: these people hunkered down and they had a process for getting it done in a deliberate and orderly fashion.

- They studied more than they typically would have
- Some studied smarter than they typically would have
- Some studied longer
- Some used our key study aids to get over certain humps. These study aids, the DVDs, the CDs, flashcard, online systems, and so on; they use that to overcome any difficulties they found in their learning process.
- Some used mentoring to get back on track, to get beyond a roadblock

For the PMP exam, there are so many different flavours of learning and it becomes very important to understand your learning style. Adapt your study plan to your learning style, stay on it and get help where you are weak.

And my final tip: don't be surprised when you find a survey after hitting the end button; because you will. And the Survey can be skipped.?   I was so paranoid of failing the exam because of the Survey, I answered everything 'yes'. Use that Survey as a time to cool your nerves, and the moment you are finished with the Survey, you will see the bright bold letters CONGRATIULATIONS, YOU HAVE PASSED THE PMP EXAM!

Celebrate! Celebrate! Celebrate! Spoil yourself. Get something! Get a present for yourself after getting that monkey off your back. Treat yourself to something good. Why? Because you absolutely deserved it. You've earned it. You've worked so hard and now you're PMP Certified, get yourself a gift, go to town, have fun with friends, celebrate, celebrate, celebrate and never look back. Stay on it! Keep your PDUs up and that takes me to my next set of tips for after the exam.

5. **After Getting PMP Certified,** my tips for you are:
    1. Stay on top of it. Don't let it fade, don't let it die. Don't let that knowledge go to waste. Use that great knowledge to help people; help others pass the exam. How about running a study group for people aspiring to get certified.
    2. Read other PMI standards
    3. Keep in touch with the PMI, information from the PMBOK and the dogma surrounding the

PMP exam, because it fades very fast. Most importantly, find value in, making it pragmatic for yourself. If you cannot make this pragmatic on your everyday projects, people will view it as a waste of time.

4. Be prepared to LEAD – Be more, do more, contribute more, change more – build those around you with this great information. Its one thing to have knowledge, but if knowledge isn't applied, it is not power. So, make your knowledge 'power!'

I hope you have enjoyed this session on 25 Power Tips for the PMP Exam. If you need coaching, mentoring or training; be sure to visit www.praizon.com to learn more about our Project Management training solutions. All the best! Pass the exam with power!

# Busy with your work?
### Don't have time to read the PMBOK® Guide

18 AUDIO CD SET
450 PAGE STUDY GUIDE
FLASHCARDS
35 HOUR TRAINING ON LMS
EMAIL MENTORING

### YOU NEED THE
## PROJECT MANAGEMENT AUDIO DIGEST

If you are busy with work and don't have time to read the PMBOK® Guide, then you need the Project Management Audio Digest: a portable study aid for the PMP® and CAPM® Exam. You can take it with you on-the-go, in your car, at the gym or on break. It is an accessible quick reference at work when you need some useful project management information.

This set includes 18 Audio CDs; an indepth 20 hour audio review of the PMBOK® Guide Fifth Edition covering all chapters with audio dramatization of the knowledge areas and process groups

### available at www.praizion.com
#### Praizion media
*Real world project management training solutions*

www.ingramcontent.com/pod-product-compliance
Lightning Source LLC
Chambersburg PA
CBHW031418040426
42444CB00005B/622